Machines at work
AEROPLANE

DK

LONDON, NEW YORK, MUNICH,
MELBOURNE and DELHI

Written and edited by Caroline Bingham
Designed by Cheryl Telfer
Managing editor Susan Leonard
Managing art editor Clare Shedden
Jacket design Emy Manby
Jacket editor Mariza O'Keeffe
Picture researcher Carolyn Clerkin
Production Lucy Baker
DTP Designer Almudena Díaz
Consultant Michael Allaby

First published in Great Britain in 2003
by Dorling Kindersley Limited.
80 Strand, London WC2R ORL

A Penguin Company
2 4 6 8 10 9 7 5 3 1

Paperback edition ISBN 1-4053-1482-6
Hardback edition ISBN 0-7513-6496-7

Colour reproduction by GRB Editrice, S.r.l., Verona, Italy
Printed and bound in China by Toppan Printing Co., Ltd

see our complete
catalogue at
www.dk.com

Contents

Getting ready

An **airport** is a busy place, with aeroplanes constantly arriving and departing. Each plane has to be checked, refuelled, and cleaned – often in less than an hour.

An international airport may see more than 200,000 passengers pass through each day.

Get ready to board

At a large airport, the planes line up at gates. This is where passengers get on and off.

In with the cargo

Scissor-lift machines are used to load and unload a large plane with all sorts of containers. Some will contain food for the flight.

More than 20 vehicles may come and go to service a large aeroplane.

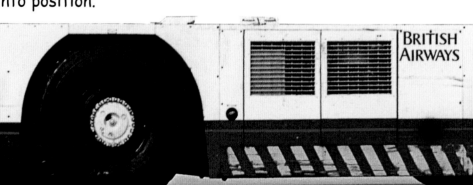

The tug driver reverses the tug into position.

The pilot talks to the tug driver by radio.

Emmly Masanabo

A little push
When a big plane is ready to leave, it is pushed away from the gate by a tug. Once in position, the pilot starts the engines and the aeroplane moves forward.

The tug's tow bar attaches to the nose wheels.

Taking off

Traffic jam

At a busy airport, aeroplanes may be flying in and out every minute. They sometimes have to line up and wait for permission to move, or taxi, onto the runway.

As an aeroplane roars down the runway, air rushes over and under the **wings** in such a way that the plane is forced up.

Wheels are drawn back into compartments in the fuselage.

Flaps are tilted down to increase the wing's curve.

A runway is often more than 3 kilometres (2 miles) in length.

Fasten your seat belts! Get ready for take off.

6

Staying in touch

When waiting to land, an aeroplane is in constant contact with the control tower. The plane will appear on the control tower's computer screens as a tiny dot.

Get ready to land.

In control

It's easy to spot an airport's control tower – it's a tall building and often a funny shape. The people inside decide when each plane can take off or land.

Up with the wheels

The wheels (or landing gear) are pulled up quickly after take off. This lowers drag – the resistance pulling against the aircraft.

Flying high

Imagine sitting at the controls of a large airliner. The panel in front of you is packed with buttons, switches, screens, lights, and dials. A **pilot** has to understand what each one does.

These dials provide information about the engine.

Which one first?

The basic flight controls – the yoke, wing flap control, and throttles – are within easy reach of the pilot and co-pilot.

Control yoke

It's a fact

🛩 The 767 flight deck was the first two- (instead of three-) person flight deck on a twin-aisle aeroplane.

🛩 Thanks to computers, modern 747s have just 365 controls. The first models had 971 flight deck controls.

Landing and taxi light switches

Screens have replaced the banks of dials in older aeroplanes.

Make way for the jumbo!

A **Boeing 747** is the largest passenger aeroplane in the world. It can carry about **400** passengers. That's why it's known as a jumbo. It's a giant among aeroplanes.

A long stretch

The top of a 747's tailfin is 19 metres (63 feet) above the ground. Maintenance workers use machines called cherry pickers to get there.

Fuel is carried in the wings, in the central section between the wings, and in the tail.

Packing it in

A fully loaded 747 will have 416 passengers on board, along with around 600 pieces of luggage in the hold, and more than 800 meals.

Where do you sit?

There are three seating areas in a typical 747 — and the more you pay, the more space you get.

747s are so big that they have a second floor – and stairs to get to it.

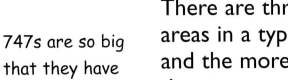

Ten passengers can sit side-by-side in the economy section.

At 19 centimetres (7 inches) thick, the fuselage skin is almost as wide as a page from this book.

It's a fact

The 36-metre (120-foot) distance of the Wright brothers' first flight could have taken place within the 45-metre (150-foot) economy section of a 747.

11

Where's the engine?

Imagine soaring through the air without the sound of an engine. That's what it's like when you fly in a **glider**.

How does it stay up?

Once in the air, a glider pilot looks for thermals – warm pockets of rising air – to climb. A glider can stay up for hours by riding these thermals.

Towing a glider is called an aero-tow.

A helping hand

A glider has to be helped into the air. One way of doing this is to drag it up behind a powered plane. A long cable connects the two aircraft and is released in the air

These acrobatic gliders can perform loop-the-loops.

A tight squeeze

Modern gliders can have wingspans that are longer than Concorde! But the cockpit is always tiny. And, as with all aeroplanes, there is a weight limit – so you have to know how much you weigh before you fly.

The world distance record for a glider is an amazing 2,463 kilometres (1,530 miles).

Thirsty beasts

Some military planes are equipped to **refuel** in midair. Picking up the hose to collect fuel takes a lot of skill.

The rim of the drogue basket inflates in the air.

Aviation fuel is pumped along the fuel line at about 4,500 litres (1,000 gallons) a minute.

A speedy exchange
The two aeroplanes fly only metres apart, but are moving three times as fast as a car on a motorway.

A steady workhorse
Aircraft chosen as tankers have to be strong and dependable. The VC-10, shown here refuelling a Tornado, is a good example. It is a converted passenger plane.

Refuelling can take place from a wing-mounted refuelling pod.

Refuelling probe

Easy does it
The pilot of the plane to be refuelled has to line up with the tanker and match the tanker's speed before attempting to hook up.

Refuelling can take from 2 to 45 minutes.

15

How does a helicopter fly?

About **500** years ago an Italian artist and scientist named Leonardo da Vinci sketched an idea for a **helicopter**. Yet the first helicopter did not fly until the **1930s**.

It has two!
The Chinook transport helicopter is powered by two engines. These turn the 18.3-metre (60-foot) diameter three-blade rotors.

Keep on spinning
Instead of wings, a helicopter has long rotor blades that spin around to pull the aircraft up into the air. They are driven by an engine above the cabin.

Helicopter rotors spin around about 500 times a minute.

Perfect for rescue

Helicopters are perfect for search and rescue in remote areas. They can hover, fly backwards, forwards, sideways, and straight up and down.

A helicopter doesn't need a runway.

C-GRNR

Metal skids instead of wheels mean this helicopter can land on unstable ground.

Air acrobats

Stunt planes are the acrobats of the air. Whether flying in groups or alone, they give an incredible display.

Aeroplanes with two wings are known as biplanes.

Leaving a trail
Aerobatic planes often release vapour trails, which stream out behind them. Sometimes these are dyed red or blue.

Wing to wing
Stunt planes flying together can make many different formations in the sky, with wingtips nearly touching.

From spin to roll to loop-the-loop.

The pilot of each plane is in constant radio contact with the other pilots in the display team.

Just taking a stroll...
Helped by a safety harness, wing walkers perform death-defying stunts on the wings of a plane.

Little flyers

A microlight is a tiny one- or two-person aircraft with a small engine and a propeller. The **pilot** sits in a trike.

Just hanging around

Microlights developed from the sport of hang gliding, where a person flies under a huge wing. Body movement controls the hang glider's direction.

A high flyer

Once up, a microlight can stay in the air for several hours, and reach about 900 metres (15,000 feet).

One microlight has managed to stay up for

A comfortable chair

The pilot sits in a small seat, on top of three fixed wheels. The wheels are needed for take off and landing. A microlight pilot wears a helmet.

The metal frame is made of lightweight aluminium.

1,071 km (665 miles).

It's a fact

Take off happens at 32 kph (20 mph).

Top speed is about 97 kph (60 mph).

A microlight can fly for about four hours.

Record breaker

This amazing aircraft first flew in the 1960s. It is known as the **Blackbird** because of its black coating and unusual shape. It is the **fastest jet** aircraft ever.

A Blackbird pilot wears a suit that is a bit like an astronaut's. It seals the pilot inside.

It's cold outside

This suit protects the pilot in case he has to eject. At the height the plane flies, the air is too thin to breathe and too cold to survive without help.

The parachute is known as a drag chute because it drags the air to slow the plane.

Stop, stop, S-T-O-P

Blackbird touches down at such a high speed that it needs help from a parachute to stop! The parachute stops the plane within about 1,000 metres (1,100 yards).

Tiny iron balls in the paint mean the plane cannot be seen on radar.

Stop that leak!

On the way up, fuel streaks out of Blackbird's tanks. Once the plane heats up, the metal expands enough to seal the tanks.

23

A watery landing

Not all aeroplanes are built to land on a hard runway. **Amphibians** and **seaplanes** land on water.

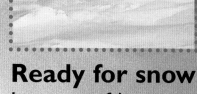

Ready for snow
In areas of heavy snow, aeroplanes can even be fitted with skis!

Echoes of a gull
This large amphibious plane is a Beriev Be-12. The gull-shaped wings are mounted at the top of the fuselage, keeping the engines clear of water spray.

The four-blade propeller is 4.85 metres (16 foot) in diameter.

The plane could reach the top of the Eiffel Tower in France in just 20 seconds.

Float on by

In areas with wide expanses of water, small four-seater passenger planes have floats instead of wheels.

Blast off!

A space shuttle roars up, leaving a massive **vapour trail** behind. It can make repeated trips to and from space, delivering and repairing **satellites.**

Made up of parts

The space shuttle is made up of four main parts. The orbiter rides on the back of a gigantic fuel tank and two booster rockets.

Take off!

The space shuttle blasts off and moves upwards, away from the launch pad. Hot gases escape from the rocket, forcing the shuttle upwards.

The huge fuel tank falls away about eight minutes into the flight.

Space for a satellite

Once in orbit, huge doors in the back of the shuttle are opened, exposing the payload bay. This is where satellites are carried into space.

An astronaut at work on the orbiter's robotic arm.

The two rocket boosters fall away about two minutes into the flight.

Hitching a lift

The orbiter is transported back to base on the back of a jumbo jet from the airport at which it lands.

A model of one of Leonardo's sketches.

Days of old

The fight to claim the skies has come a long way since the first **powered** flight by the Wright brothers' *Flyer*, which took place on 17 December 1903.

First attempts

Leonardo da Vinci (1452-1519) spent many hours sketching bird and bat flight. He also sketched ideas for fabric-winged flying machines.

The S.E.5a could reach 222 kph (138 mph).

Wright Flyer

Wilbur and Orville Wright were fascinated by flight from a young age. Their *Flyer* flew just four times before it crashed and was destroyed, but it was an incredible achievement. Five people witnessed the 12-second flight.

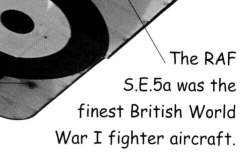

The RAF S.E.5a was the finest British World War I fighter aircraft.

Getting bigger

The Lockheed Constellation shows how quickly aircraft developed. By the 1950s, Constellations were carrying 99 passengers across ocean routes at cruising speeds of 526 kph (327 mph).

Each engine had more than 200 times the power of the **Flyer**.

A biplane has two wings and an open cockpit.

It's a fact

🐦 The **Flyer** had a 12-hp engine. A modern family car has an engine that is ten times as powerful.

🐦 Biplanes took to the skies in huge numbers in World War I (1914-1918).

One wing or two?

Biplanes are an important stage in the history of flight. Early planes had thin wood and fabric wings. Struts and bracing wire between two wings increased their strength.

Picture gallery

Blackbird

To heat their food, Blackbird pilots held the packets against the hot cockpit windows.

Seaplane

A seaplane's runway is the water. A small seaplane needs about 1.6 km (1 mile) of clear water on which to land.

Glider

The world altitude record for a glider is just under 15,000 metres (50,000 feet).

Space shuttle

There are four space shuttles. Each was designed to fly 100 missions.

Biplane

A biplane's open cockpit means the pilot needs a warm hat, scarf, gloves, jacket – and goggles.

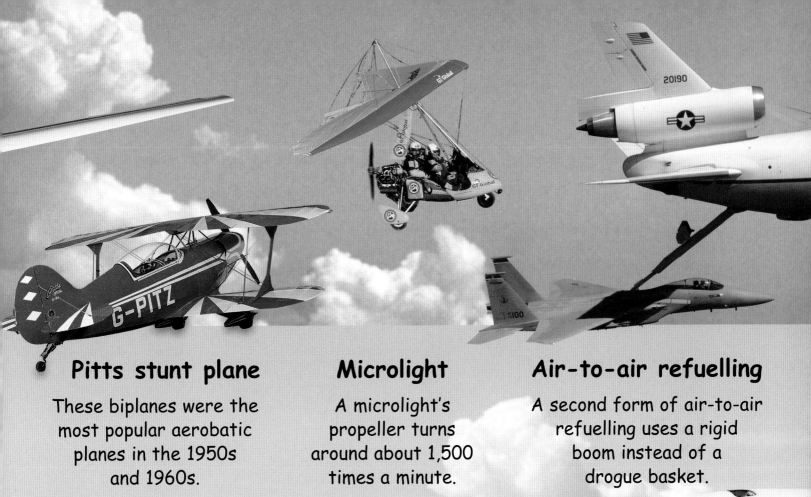

Pitts stunt plane

These biplanes were the most popular aerobatic planes in the 1950s and 1960s.

Microlight

A microlight's propeller turns around about 1,500 times a minute.

Air-to-air refuelling

A second form of air-to-air refuelling uses a rigid boom instead of a drogue basket.

Emmly Masanabo

Chinook

There are about 300 control buttons and switches on the flight deck of this Chinook.

Jumbo jet

You could park 45 family-sized cars on the wings of a jumbo jet.

Glossary

Amphibian is an aeroplane that can operate on land and water.

Control tower is a tall airport building. The people inside direct the aircraft flying into and out of the airport.

Flight deck is the cockpit of the aeroplane where the pilot and co-pilot operate the flight controls.

Fuselage is the main body of an aeroplane that holds the crew, passengers, and luggage.

Orbiter is the spacecraft part of a space shuttle; the part that holds the astronauts.

Payload bay is the part of the orbiter that holds the satellite or other equipment needed for a mission.

Propeller is the rotating blade on some aircraft. The propellers are driven by the engine and power the plane through the air.

Runway is a strip of ground where aeroplanes can take off or land.

Thermals are rising bodies of warm air. A glider uses thermals to stay up.

Throttle is a mechanism on the flight deck that controls the flow of fuel to the plane's engines, which allows the pilot to control his speed.

Vapour trail is the visible stream released behind an aeroplane. The stream is water vapour.

Yoke is the control device on the flight deck that the pilot and co-pilot use to steer the plane.

Index

Airliner coming in to land

Acknowledgements

Dorling Kindersley would like to thank:
Fleur Star for preparing the index and assisting with the glossary; and Rebecca Sodergren for picture library services.

Picture credits:

The publisher would like to thank the following for their kind permission to reproduce their photographs:

a=above; c=center; b=below; l=left; r=right; t=top;
1: Richard Cooke; 2-3: Richard Cooke; 4: Corbis/Kevin Fleming tl; Robert Harding Picture Library crb; 4-5: Austin Brown/Aviation Picture Library; 6: Corbis/Kevin Fleming tl; 6-7: Corbis/ George Hall; 7: Aviation Images tl; 7: Getty photodisc/Jack Hollingsworth cra; 8-9: The Flight Collection; 10: Corbis/Adrian Carroll/Eye Ubiquitous tl; 10-11: Corbis/Eric Curry; 11: Austin Brown/Aviation Picture Library tr; 12: Austin Brown/Aviation Picture Library br; ; 12-13: Austin Brown/Aviation Picture Library; 13: Airsport Photo Library/Guy Westgate tr; 14: Aviation Images/John Dibbs cl; Aviation Images/Mark Wagner br; 14-15: Corbis/Chris Simpson/Cordaiy Photo Library Ltd; 16: Aviation Images/Mark Wagner bl; 16-17: Getty Images/Jean A.E.F.Duboisberranger; 18-19: Corbis/James A. Sugar; 19: Corbis/Bettmann cr; Robert Harding Picture Library/Ian Griffiths tc; 20: Corbis/Bob Krist tl; Corbis/Tim Wright cl; 20-21: Corbis/Paul A. Souders;. 21: Corbis/Tim Wright r; 22: Aviation Images tr; Corbis cr; 23: Aviation Images; 24: Robert Harding Picture Library tr; 24-25: Aviation Images/Mark Wagner; 26: NASA cl; 26-27: NASA c, b; 27: NASA cr, br; 28: Corbis cl; 28-29: Aviation Images/John Dibbs c; Richard Cooke t; 29: Aviation Images/Mark Wagner cra; 30: Aviation Images tl; Aviation Images/John Dibbs br; Corbis/Carol Havers tc; Corbis/Joseph Sohm/ChromoSohm Inc tr; NASA bl; 31: Austin Brown/Aviation Picture Library tc, br; Corbis/George Hall tr; 32: Corbis/David Lawrence bl; eps: alamy.com/ Steve Bloom Images; Jacket: front main picture: FTOP Pte. Ltd., Singapore Colin Koh; back cover background shot: FTOP Pte. Ltd., Singapore

All other images © Dorling Kindersley
For further information see: www.dkimages.com